loved

THE LORD'S PRAYER

SALLY
LLOYD-JONES
AND JAGO

ZONDERKIDZ

Loved

Copyright © 2007 by Sally Lloyd-Jones
Illustrations © 2018 by Jago

This edition ISBN: 978-0-310-76944-6

Requests for information should be addressed to:
Zonderkidz, 3900 *Sparks Drive SE, Grand Rapids, Michigan 49546*

All Scripture quotations, unless otherwise indicated, are taken from
The Holy Bible, New International Version®, NIV®. Copyright © 1973, 1978,
1984, 2011 by Biblica, Inc.® Used by permission. All rights reserved worldwide.

Zonderkidz is a trademark of Zondervan.

Design: Brooke Reynolds

Printed in China

19 20 21 22 23 /DSC/ 6 5 4 3 2 1

Dedication

For Harry, Olivia, Emily, Eleanor and Jonathan

Because the Fairy Tale really does come true!

SLJ

For my lovely family, the best

wife, daughter, and son in the world.

All the best,

Jago

Hello Daddy!
We want to know you.

And be close to you.
Please show us how.

Make everything in the world right again.
And in our hearts too.

Do what is best—
just like you do in heaven,

and please do it down here too.

Please give us everything we need today.

Forgive us for doing wrong,
for hurting you.

Forgive us just as we forgive other people when they hurt us.

Rescue us! We need you.
We don't want to keep running away
and hiding from you.

Keep us safe from our enemies.

You're strong, God.

You can do whatever you want.

You are in charge.

Now and forever and for always!

We think you're great!
Amen!
Yes we do!

THE LORD'S PRAYER

Matthew 6:9-13

"This, then, is how you should pray:

"'Our Father in heaven,
hallowed be your name,
your kingdom come,
your will be done,
    on earth as it is in heaven.
  Give us today our daily bread.
And forgive us our debts,
    as we also have forgiven our debtors.
And lead us not into temptation,
    but deliver us from the evil one.'"